Little Book
of Crap

The
Little Book
of Crap

Dr Neil Manson

BOXTREE

First published 1999 by Boxtree
an imprint of Macmillan Publishers Ltd, 25 Eccleston Place,
London SW1W 9NF, Basingstoke and Oxford

www.macmillan.co.uk

Associated companies throughout the world

ISBN 0 7522 1824 7

9 8

A CIP catalogue record for this book is available from the
British Library.

Designed by Nigel Davies Printed by Omnia Books Ltd

I hear it all the time: 'What will *The Little Book of Crap* do for *me*? Will this tiny book *make it safe to fly*? Will it tighten up my *flabby bits* and make *everybody love me, always*?' Of course it will. It will do all these things and much more besides. As we all know, today's all-too-hasty world of fast cars and slow celebrities makes us tense, nervous, and full of fear. Strike back! Take control! Put the 'welcome' mat back in front of the door of your life. Right here, right now. It's time for *The Little Book of Crap*.

BARKING MAD

Don't worry if your family
have all been killed. A little
dab of rose water will soon
see you feeling calm again.

PROBLEM SHARING

Tell your problems to a friend.
Soon everyone will know your
business.

HOT AIR

Speak your worries into a
balloon as you inflate it.
Pop the balloon.
In all likelihood,
your worries will be gone.

SWAPSHOP

The sound of the human
heartbeat is one of the most
relaxing sounds around. Swap
that expensive discman for a
cheap stethoscope.

LUCK

See a penny, pick it up. All
day long, you'll have a penny.

FENG SHITE

Place a shiny pebble in a
wooden bowl in the corner of
your room. Who knows, it
may induce a sense of calm.

11

MONEY

They say that money talks.
But remember, dolphins sing.

BE POPULAR

Popular people have lots of
friends.

WHY SO STILL?

Dancing is very therapeutic.
If you are at a funeral,
and feel distressed, simply
start dancing.
In all probability, almost
everyone will soon join in.

STORM IN A TEACUP

Dribble your worries into a
beaker or cup. Knock it over.
Chances are your worries will
be soaked up into the carpet.

TRANSFORMATION

Put a pair of sunglasses on.
You will then surely see things
in a different light.

ROAR POWER

Pretend you are a big fierce
tiger. Now go up to someone
who has been bullying you
and give a huge roar!
It's g-r-r-reat to be the one in
charge for a change.

LIGHT THERAPY

Invest in a powerful
theatrical spotlight.
When you shine it on yourself
at home you will feel
like a star.

FANTASISE A LITTLE

If you feel muddle-headed and incapable, pretend you're clear-headed and able. It will make a world of difference.

RAINBOW WARRIOR

Bright colours can lift your spirits. Paint your room red, orange, yellow, green, blue, indigo or violet.

THE KEY TO SUCCESS

If you really, really want
something, make plans, try
hard, and you never know,
you might just succeed.

DIPLOMACY

Look at life as if it were a
game. When you're losing,
kick over the board and feign
illness. That way you'll never
come last.

ROUTINE IS GOOD

Try to stick to your routine. It
will make you feel calm.

ROUTINE IS BAD

Try to vary your routine. It
will spice up your life.

HOLDING BACK THE YEARS

Many people worry when
they reach the age of 40.
Say to yourself, 'I'm 25!'
before each meal, and relish
your new-found youth.

BACK-SEAT DRIVING

Driving can be stressful.
For a change, sit in the back
seat. Relax. Then spend a few
minutes wondering why the
car isn't moving.

THE CLEVER FINGER

Pick your nose.
Place your index finger up
your nose. You'll be amazed
at what you can find.

IT'S A DOG'S LIFE

Pretend to be a dog.
Act like a dog, bark like a dog.
And in no time at all,
people will be throwing you
dog-biscuits.

SHOULDERS BACK!

Have you ever seen how
soldiers stand proud?
Join them. Walk tall.
Keep a straight back.
But watch out for snipers.

CARRY A PIECE OF THE QUILT

Carry a piece of your duvet or other bedding. It will remind you of sleep. Happy dreams. Zzzzzzzzzzzzzzzzzzzzzzzzzz.

WASTE SOME PAPER

Top executives never waste
time mindlessly crumpling up
paper. Try it. See them turn
green with envy.

WHITE GOODS ARE GOOD FOR YOU

Buy a fridge.
Keep your food in it.
You'll soon forget that you
ever tasted soured milk.

TIME IS ON YOUR SIDE

Make sure that all your
engagements are unimportant.
That way it won't matter if
you're late.

NATURE'S WAY

Squirrels and birds don't
worry about the future.
They're happy!
Live in the present!
Live in a tree or a bush.

LIGHTS OUT

At the end of a stressful day,
turn off the lights, close your
eyes, bump into the furniture
as you do essential chores.

THAT SINKING FEELING

When things are really getting
on top of you, take some soft
cushions, listen to some
whale-song and wonder
how you ended up in the
mid-Atlantic.

PAN PIPES

Sit down, get comfortable,
breathe slowly through your
nose. Perhaps you can hear a
thin whistling.
Does it sound like pan pipes?
Probably not.

TEA

If everybody spent their days
drinking herbal tea, there
would be no time for war.
Hey presto. World Peace.

36

MORE TEA

You can't hold a teacup and a
gun in your hand.

YET MORE TEA

There's a T in togetherness,
but no T in war.

EAST, WEST, ZEST IS BEST

Put the zest back in your life
by eating some lemon rind.

TRUE ROMANCE

Don't worry if you think
your wife is having an affair.
She probably is.

CAREFREE MOMENTS

If no one cares about you, no
one will care if you're late.
Enjoy those extra minutes!

STATING THE OBVIOUS

Spend a whole day stating the
obvious. Enjoy the looks you get.

WORRY LINES

If you are stressed, write
down your worries in pencil.
Then erase everything. There.
That feels good, doesn't it.

MODERN TIMES

Television today is violent
and full of filth. If you don't
like it, try polishing, or
making jam.

SILENT NIGHT

If you find yourself fretting
about insomnia, don't worry.
Relax. Go to sleep.

MENTAL AGILITY

If you're feeling down, stand
on your head. What was
down is now up.

TAKE CONTROL

If someone is bullying you at
work, draw a picture of their
face on a piece of paper.
Place the piece of paper
on the ground and
stamp on it repeatedly.
It is unlikely that they will
ever bully you again.

43

YOU ARE WHAT YOU EAT

Eat good food and before you
know it, you'll be good.

RED CROSS CODE

If you're worried about
crossing a busy road,
pretend the cars aren't there.
Now it's safe to cross.

PROTECT YOUR PEACE

If you hear shouts for help, ignore them. They'll soon go away.

LET IT RING

If the phone rings in the middle of the night, ignore it. Enjoy the extra time you will have awake worrying.

MAN'S BEST FRIEND

Learn to love your worries
like you love your dog. After
all, worries are for life, not
just for Christmas.

PRETEND IT'S TUESDAY
AFTERNOON

TINKLE TINKLE

If you're worried about
money, don't forget that your
soul needs feeding too.
Buy some wind chimes.
Enjoy them.

LET THEM SHOW YOU THE WAY

Go swimming. After all, have you
ever seen an anxious dolphin?

WHAT EVERY
SAILOR KNOWS

A boat can't sink if it's on
dry land.

STRICTLY FOR THE BIRDS

Legend has it that Icarus
was killed because he flew
too close to the sun.
If he hadn't tried to fly, he
might still be alive today.
Don't try anything and you
won't have a nasty fall.

49

PEAK PRACTICE

If you're going on a
mountaineering holiday,
don't bother with expensive
equipment, after all ancient
wisdom has it that the
world is flat.

SELF-HEMP

Cultivate marijuana.
When you smoke it, it will
affect the neurochemicals
in your brain to make you
feel good.

CHOO CHOO, IT'S JUST YOU

Buy yourself a model train set
and an engine driver's hat.
Lonely play can induce a sense
of peace.

PUMPKIN

Stay up late.
On the stroke of midnight,
who knows you may have a
stroke of genius.

DEAD OR ALIVE

Imagine yourself on a wanted
poster. There. Somebody
wants you now. It's good to be
wanted, but not for murder.

I LIKE THE COFFEE ONES

Smile. Like chocolates, your
teeth are made for sharing.

STAMP IT OUT

If you are facing some
insurmountable difficulty,
write it down on the back
of a postage stamp and
stick the stamp on a letter
to a stranger. There!
Your problem is licked.

IS IT SAFE?

Yes.

IS IT SAFE?

No.

IS IT SAFE?

Remove the 'best before' labels from your food. Now you can enjoy the thrill and danger of eating.

THAT SINKING FEELING

Sink into a soft armchair.
But don't sink too far.
You may find it difficult to get up.

TREE HOUSE

Set up home with a tree.
You can make love to it and it
will help you feel calm.

I WANT IT
AND I WANT IT ...
NOW

If you see something that
you want in a shop window
that is way too expensive for
you, make a quick sketch
of the object of your desire
and take it home.
That'll do nicely.

SMELLS GOOD

Burn incense. Burn money.
It may help you.

TING!

Sleep with a light bulb under
your pillow. By morning you
will have had a bright idea.

JUST DO IT

Be calm.
You can't feel stressed when
you're feeling calm

CUCKOO

If you're broke, don't worry. Use
toy money, or pretty shells.

MAD FOR IT

If it is all becoming
too much for you, settle deep
into your unconscious.
There is an escape and
comfort in insanity.

ME MYSELF I

If you feel you are
self-obsessed,
take a self-help course
to confirm your belief.

ROLL OVER

If you find that you feel
threatened by your work
colleagues, imagine they
are all little puppies.
Who's top dog now?

THAT'S ALL RIGHT THEN

Many people are ashamed
of their bodies.
There is no need.
After all your body is not
ashamed of you.

TOPTASTIC

Move to the North Pole.
You'll feel on top of the world.

HAT-TRICK

Wear an over-sized hat. No one
will call you big-headed again.

ENJOY YOURSELF, IT'S LATER THAN YOU THINK.

ADVICE SLIP

Money worries may be
overcome by taking a second job.

PLATFORM SHOOS

If you are waiting on a crowded platform and your train is late, don't become angry. Sing old glam-rock songs at the top of your voice, and soon you'll have plenty of space to relax and view the crowds around you.

WHAT PROBLEM?

Practice makes perfect.
Practise denial. Nothing will
ever go wrong.

VEG OUT

Don't eat raw vegetables. Raw
is an anagram of war.

LOAD OF BALLS

Put your cigarettes inside a
football. Now it will be easy
to kick the habit.

A LITTLE PORKY

If you have a chronic disease
write its name on a piece of
ham. Now it's cured.

AS EASY AS ABC

Write down a list of your
worries. Put them into
alphabetical order. Now you
have them sorted. Well done.

SAND ADVICE

Stick your head in the sand.
The worst thing that can
happen now is that you get
sand in your eyes.

WHO'S SORRY NOW?

If someone tries to trick you
out of a prized possession,
turn the tables on them by
giving them whatever it is that
they want. Enjoy watching the
expression on their face!
The last laugh will be yours
to savour.

LOOK AT THE SIZE OF IT

If you are embarrassed
by some part of your body,
confront it, draw everyone's
attention to it, talk
about it incessantly.
Your embarrassment will
soon disappear.

LOAD OF OLD COBBLERS

Try to get a job as a cobbler.
There is no pleasure like the
pleasure of fixing someone
else's sole.

HAVE YOU PAID FOR THOSE, MADAM?

Help others to help
themselves. But not if you're
a store detective.

BLOW YOUR OWN TRUMPET

Listen to free-form jazz.
Rejoice in the knowledge that
your life isn't that chaotic.

MY LEFT FOOT

Enjoy a day hopping on your
right foot. Your left foot will
enjoy a well-earned rest.

THE TRUTH

Even your shadow needs time
to itself, away from you and
your sadness.

BEEN THERE, DONE THAT

The only things
worth achieving are the things
you've done already.

OR DID THEY?

Dance and shriek like a
Neanderthal man.
After all, they never
worried about mortgages
and inflation.

JUST BECAUSE YOU'RE BETTER THAN ME, DOESN'T MEAN I'M LAZY

If you are mediocre,
make sure that you work with
talented, successful people.
Bask in the reflected glory.

IT COULD BE YOU

Be lucky on the lottery.
Everybody will love your win-
ning ways.

IF YOU LOVE SOMEBODY
— SET THEM FREE.

HOME JAMES

Offer to drive on
the night of your office party.
Everyone will be
transported by your
generosity.

FLOWER POWER

Put some lilies in a china vase
on top your television. From
now on, there will always be
something on TV.

MY, HOW YOU'VE GROWN

If you lose custody of your child, don't worry, you'll be able to see them in the school holidays.

SPARE ANY CHANGE?

Change can be good as well as
bad. Look on the bright side if
you lose your job.

ONLY YOU

Remember, no matter what
anyone says, there is only one
person that is you.

TWINKLE TWINKLE

Put on a pointy hat.
Stand with your legs apart
and your arms outstretched.
You will feel like a star.

EXCUSE ME

Don't be shy.
Go out and speak
to strangers.

DAILY UNDERTAKING

Every morning, imagine that
you're dead. There.
You can't feel more at peace
than that.

I'M OUTTA HERE

When you have a stressful
problem, run away from it.
Fast as you can.

WHERE THERE'S NO WILL THERE'S A WAY

Lower your standards to the
level you're at. Success is easy.

LEAF IT OUT

Get lots of money. Then you can
avoid the city, the strain, and go
for a long country walk.

A FRIEND IN NEED IS A FRIEND INDEED

If you want to feel loved,
make friends with the lonely
and desperate.

EVERY ONE'S A WINNER BABY

If you have low self-esteem,
remember, everyone is better
than someone else.

GOING UP!

If you're depressed from
living in a tower block,
put a bottle of whisky
in the elevator. Everyday,
your spirits will be lifted.

WHO'S THE FAIREST OF THEM ALL?

If you're worried about
your fading looks,
put a picture of your favourite
film star on the mirror.

LIFE'S A BEACH

Get shipwrecked and spend
the rest of your life in lonely
solitude on a desert island.
Then you will be calm.

JUST RESTING

Look for the positive if you can.
If you lose your job, don't worry,
the change of routine may
induce a sense of calm.

PLAN A

Don't make plans, be free.
Plans are a straightjacket.

PLAN B

Don't be anxious, make plans.
Plans help you to organise
your life and reduce stress.

PLAN NINE
FROM OUTER SPACE

Befriend an alien.
He will probably
fix your bike,
and other good things.

HAPPY CLAPPY

Clap your hands
when someone has done
something good.
Many believe that it is a sign
of appreciation.

NOT WAVING, DROWNING

Pretend that you're a traffic policeman. Enjoy the feeling of excitement and power as you wave the traffic on.

FOOT THE BILL

Don't waste money on
expensive shoes.
Cheap sandals will do.

CAN'T, SHAN'T, WON'T

It is better to give up
than to risk failure.

YOU CRACK ME UP

Don't worry if you never
get jokes and don't have
a sense of humour.
Pretend that you get it.
Then laugh louder than
everyone else.

GAME ON

Become addicted to
computer games.
They soak up all the time
available so that you
won't have any life to feel
worried about.

LOOK ON THE BRIGHT SIDE

When there is a cloud
on the horizon, take heart.
Rain is necessary to water
your garden.

CLOUD CUCKOO LAND

Remember every cloud
has a silver lining, and you
can use silver to buy
whatever you want.

KEEP ON RUNNIN'

Train to be an athlete.
Now you really can run away
from your problems.

SEXY

Solve all your problems by
wearing exotic underwear.

YOU'LL NEVER GET IT OFF THE GROUND

Cynics may say that you can't get absolutely everything that you want, all the time. But remember, they said that man would never fly. We all know about the Wright Brothers. Soon you may get everything you want after all!

GOING, GOING ...

Get up. Give up.
It's so easy to find peace.

... GONE

Everything is fine as it is.
Now go back to sleep.

SAGE STUFFING

Some people like to say
'If it ain't broken don't fix it'.
The wise man says
'If it is broken, don't try to fix it.
Just relax!'

114

DESIGNER IMAGE

Save money – buy cheap
and shoddy goods and
pretend that you can see
expensive labels on the items
that you buy.

MENTAL ASPIRIN

If you have a throbbing
headache ignore the pain.
Your headache will soon be a
thing of the past.

HOUSE OF CORRECTION

If people all agree that you are
wrong about something, just
say to them, fairly but firmly
'No! You are.' Doesn't it feel
good to be right?

117

THE GENTLE TOUCH

Flesh feels good to the touch.
Get a part-time job
in an abattoir.

SING HOSANNA!

If your stereo doesn't work
just sing your favourite songs.
Or whistle them.
Blowing out air can make you
feel very light.

GO BANANAS

If you cannot sleep, put
bananas in your bed. You may
find the smell very restful.

BARE CHEEK

Go to work naked once in a
while. Now people will really
sit up and notice.

MINE'S A PINT

The pessimist says that the
glass is half-empty, the
optimist that it is half-full.
The wise man pretends that
the glass is full. Cheers!

HELLO ... HELLO

If you are lonely,
go to the hills and shout!
Your echo will keep
you company for days.
Or weeks.

IS IT ME YOU'RE LOOKING FOR?

Remember the fun you had as
a child playing hide and seek.
Why not go and hide
somewhere now.
It will probably be ages before
anyone finds you!

DOIN' THE
LAMBETH WALK

If you are short of cash,
fill your pockets with
washers and nails.
You will feel like a
'million dollars' as you stroll
chinking along.

MAKE FRIENDS WITH A TAX CONSULTANT

Or someone else who may be
able to help you for free.

PEARLS
OF WISDOM

Do whatever you want, unless
there is some reason not to.

AND FINALLY, CYRIL ...

Buy a self-help book,
rage at the shit in it,
and then feel happy that
you're not a loser who
plays on human misery by
peddling the literary
equivalent of methadone.